The journey

Kate Hayes

The journey of the Son

An individual or small group Bible resource from Scripture Union

© Copyright Kate Hayes 2004

Scripture Union, 207–209 Queensway, Bletchley, MK2 2EB, England
Email: info@scriptureunion.org.uk
Website: www.scriptureunion.org.uk

Scripture Union Australia
Locked Bag 2, Central Coast Business Centre, NSW 2252
Website: www.su.org.au

Scripture Union USA
P.O. Box 987, Valley Forge, PA 19482
Website: www.scriptureunion.org   .

First published 2004
ISBN 1 84427 097 1

Scripture taken from the New Living Translation, British text, published by Tyndale House Publishers, Inc, Wheaton, Illinois, USA, and distributed by STL Ltd, Carlisle, Cumbria, England.

British Library Cataloguing-in-Publication Data: a catalogue record for this book is available from the British Library.

Cover design by Philip Grundy.
Typeset by Servis Filmsetting Ltd.
Printed and bound by Interprint of Malta.

✆ Scripture Union is an international Christian charity working with churches in more than 130 countries providing resources to bring the good news about Jesus Christ to children, young people and families – and to encourage them to develop spiritually through the Bible and prayer.

As well as our network of volunteers, staff and associates who run holidays, church-based events and school Christian groups, we produce a wide range of publications and support those who use our resources through training programmes.

The way ahead

*T*his book is a companion to any individual or small group wanting to grow in their understanding of Jesus' journey, and our own. Think of it more as a map book than a recipe book. No two individuals will have the same journey, though some will find themselves on paths that others have travelled. It's good to meet fellow pilgrims along the way and learn from each other.

Some will be travelling with light hearts. They are discovering a growing intimacy with the Father they love; they sense they are heard, affirmed, encouraged. They feel a response to the cries of their hearts. Others are stumbling along a different path. The ground is stony; there are obstructions and diversions. They feel alone, unheard, ignored. Their hearts ache for even a murmur of response. But the silence is deafening. They feel lost, anxious that they have wandered off track.

Take courage! As we follow in the footsteps of Jesus we see he was a fellow traveller walking the same stony paths as we do. In his journey of faith we find help with our own journeys: a guide in the face of the challenges along the path and a signpost showing us the way to our final destination.

Let us travel together for a while, share our hearts, and seek his answering voice together. It may be that we shall discover other ways of listening, other ways of hearing, and that the diversions and roadblocks are indeed part of the map.

The Solitary Pilgrim

This book is a companion for the solitary traveller. You can work through the material at your own pace, ignoring only those sections marked with the group logo. It may be helpful for you to record your thoughts along the way, either on the pages or in a separate notebook.

The Group of Pilgrims

This book is also a companion for a small group. You may have come together with a Christian friend, as a prayer triplet, as an existing small fellowship group. Or you may be part of a group specially convened for Lent or some other season of the year. Decide whether one person will lead each time you meet, or whether a different person will lead each session. You may want to skip those sections marked with the solitary pilgrim logo.

Using the material

The material is divided into six sessions or chapters, and there is a consistent pattern to the material in each.

Setting Out will ease you gently into the focus of the session, often with some fun questions. Don't skip this part, even if you are a solitary pilgrim, because however light this material seems it will flag up some important attitudes and preconceptions and will prepare you for deeper exploration of some key issues. Within the group setting, this opening time will develop relationships and encourage honest sharing which will ultimately benefit the group's ease in praying together.

Signposts will take you into the Bible. This time of discovery alone or together will open up a number of lines of thought as you follow through the questions. For groups, this section will particularly facilitate discussion and the sharing of experience.

Prayer is the next section, during which time there is opportunity to pray appropriately and in a way which is directly informed by the session so far. Don't be tempted to rush this; it is not optional but key.

Some chapters contain an **En Route** section. This contains ideas for responses or activities which will not necessarily be completed in the session but over a period of time. These may begin as exercises which, if they prove helpful, can be adopted longer term. Select only what seems helpful to you. For groups this section is something individuals might like to take away and try. But don't forget in subsequent sessions to give opportunity for reporting back.

Finally, there is a **Further Afield** section. This allows further exploration in the Bible. Depending on the length of your times together, groups wanting a longer Bible study section could use some or all of this material in the **Signposts** section. If time is limited, group members might like to take home **Further Afield** for personal study during the week. Individuals can choose to use some or all of this section. Working through it will really add breadth to your overall experience of **The journey of the Son**.

1 *Taking the plunge*

Waiting for a new stage in life can be hugely exciting; a time of looking forward to new challenges and demands, sometimes even to new places and people. New challenges are not always wholly good news though, are they? As we leap into the unknown we can find ourselves with other, less welcome, emotions too; the fear that keeps us awake in the early hours or brings a churning stomach, the doubts that see us questioning a decision. What if it all goes wrong? How will people react if we can't do it? Would we be better to stay as we are and not to try at all?

Here we begin our journey with Jesus at the moment when he makes a leap into the unknown; abandoning the relative calm of an ordinary carpenter's life in Nazareth for the turbulent route to death on the cross.

Setting Out

For each situation, choose the response that is most like you.

1 You need to write a thank you note for a Christmas present. Do you:
   a Write the letter before you open any more presents?
   b Make sure it's in the post by the New Year?
   c Take several weeks to get round to it and have to start by apologising for the delay?
   d Buy some pre-printed thank you cards and just stick one of them in an envelope?
   e Decide that if they can't buy you a better present they don't deserve a thank you anyway?

2 You've invited some friends for a meal and have refused their offer to wash up. Do you:
   a Whip the plates away as they lift their last forkful and wash up between each course?
   b Leave it for now but make sure it's done before you go to bed?
   c Do it as and when you need the plates or pans for something else?
   d Ring them up the next morning and ask them if they'd mind calling after work and washing up after all?
   e Bin everything and go shopping for replacements?

3 At work, you find you've been volunteered to give a presentation to some clients next month. Do you:

    a Cancel everything and spend every spare minute for the next month planning it?

    b Do it in little bits here and there over the next month?

    c Leave it. If you do it the night before it'll be fresh in your mind the next day?

    d Bribe a colleague to prepare it for you?

    e Pretend everything's under control then ring in sick?

4 An acquaintance is having an operation in hospital and you've offered to visit them while they're there. Do you:

    a Turn up every day with magazines, grapes and lots of interesting things to say?

    b Remember with a panic that they're due out tomorrow and have to rush to get there before visiting ends, buying the last bunch of wilting flowers from the hospital shop on the way?

    c Remember with a panic that they came out today and visit them at home instead?

    d Remember your offer when you see them walking round the supermarket a few weeks later?

    e Wonder why they're disappointed you didn't turn up, you were just being polite?

5 In the notices you hear that your church is starting up a new ministry among the homeless and you'd really like to be involved. Do you:

    a Offer to get involved but drop out when you find they need helpers, not someone to take overall charge?

    b Make sure you don't go home after the service until your name is on that list of helpers?

    c Go home dithering and decide that they don't really want ordinary people like you to help, do they?

    d Decide that if God really wants you to get involved they'll approach you?

    e Remember the thought when you see the ministry has had to stop for lack of volunteer helpers?

Q: Do your answers suggest you are more likely to get on with something straight away, wait until the last moment or avoid things altogether? Is that fair?

Q: What do you think are the advantages of a 'let's do it' approach? What are the disadvantages?

Q: What about a 'wait and see' attitude? What's good or bad about that?

Signposts

We all need wisdom to know when it's best to wait, to plunge in or to try a different route altogether. Jesus didn't plunge into ministry the moment he reached adulthood; instead he lived quietly in Nazareth until he was 30. Was that time in Nazareth wasted or did it have a purpose? Why do you think that?

THE TIME IS COMING

Read

Matthew 3:1–12

Q: John's preaching is stirring things up. How would you sum up his message?

Q: Why is he preaching such a message now?

Q: When people come to hear him, he baptises some of them. What does this baptism show?

Q: John wouldn't baptise just anybody; he refused the Pharisees and Sadducees. What was the difference between those he did baptise and those he didn't?

THE WAITING ENDS

Read

Matthew 3:13–17

Q: The years of waiting are over. What do you think made Jesus decide it was time to leave Nazareth?

[A map will show that Jesus had to make a deliberate choice to go out and find John at the Jordan River. He didn't just bump into him and choose to be baptised on the spur of the moment.]

Q: Do you like the process of travelling? How do you feel before you set out on a long journey?

Q: How do you think Jesus might have felt as he left his home and set out to find John?

Q: Waiting had been important, but now Jesus had to leave his familiar surroundings and do something different for God's plan to be fulfilled. Like Jesus, we find ourselves in situations where we have to choose whether to step out and obey God or not. Can you think of a time when you faced such a moment? Did you make the right choice or not? How did you decide what to do?

Q: Jesus didn't just plunge in but waited patiently for the right time to act. How can we be like Jesus and follow God's timing?

Q: Are you in a situation where you aren't sure whether to wait or to act at the moment? How could other people help you know what God wants you to do? If you are meeting with a group perhaps you could share something of that situation with them and pray together for God's direction.

JESUS' BAPTISM

Imagine some important information needs passing to everyone in your local community. Perhaps the bin men are coming 24 hours early or the water is going to be cut off all weekend. How many different ways can you think of to spread that information around your community quickly?

Jesus certainly had an important message for people but no modern technology to help him share it, and at this stage no disciples either. He could have made a quick impact on a lot of people if he had gone straight to the Temple in Jerusalem and started speaking and performing miracles there. Why do you think he didn't do that?

Jesus avoids a dramatic high-profile beginning to his ministry, choosing to go well away from the glare of the Temple authorities in Jerusalem and find John at the Jordan River.

Q: How do you respond when you're asked to do something and you can't see a good reason for doing it?

Q: John didn't see why Jesus wanted John to baptise him. Why did he object? What made him change his mind?

Q: Jesus didn't have any sins to be forgiven but he still said it was right for him to be baptised. Why was it so important?

GOD'S RESPONSE TO JESUS

At the beginning of his ministry, Jesus' baptism makes two things clear:

1 He is going to do exactly what God wants him to do.
2 He isn't playing at being our Saviour; he identifies completely with us as sinners.

In return for his obedience, God anointed Jesus with his Spirit (v 16) and reminded him of two things:

1 He was God's beloved Son (v 17).
2 He had God's approval (v 17).

Q: Why might Jesus have found it good to hear these things as he began his ministry?

Q: How might such a reassurance have helped him later on when things got tough?

Read

Romans 6:16

Q: Receiving God's approval didn't bring Jesus lots of money or a soft life. What does it mean for us?

Q: Paul says that if we obey God then, like Jesus, we receive God's approval. How does that make you feel?

Prayer

Begin with a time of reflection.

Groups may like to have one person read out the following, whilst the others listen, allowing time for reflection at appropriate moments.

Every day we face the same choice as Jesus; shall I choose to do what God wants or not?

Which choice did you make today?

What shows that?

In the quiet, ask God to show you whether you are living in obedience to him or not. Is there something he wants you to change, perhaps to do something you've neglected or to give something up?

Ask God to forgive you for the times you've chosen to go your own way rather than his, perhaps using a prayer from a book you use, or these words from Psalm 86:

Teach me your ways, O LORD, that I may live according to your truth!
Grant me purity of heart, that I may honour you.
With all my heart I will praise you, O Lord my God.
I will give glory to your name forever,
for your love for me is very great.
You have rescued me from the depths of death!
Psalm 86:11–13

Every moment of every day is a choice, to go God's way or our own. Pray that you will have the strength and the courage to choose God's way this week.

Further Afield

1 RELUCTANT OBEDIENCE

Read

Exodus 3 and 4, particularly 3:1–10; 4:10–13,27–31

Q: Surprises. Do you love them or hate them?

Q: Moses is calmly going about his business when God surprises him. Do you think Moses enjoyed his surprise or not?

Q: Most of us have at least some plans and expectations of how things are going to turn out in life, whether concerning big things or small, but our plans aren't necessarily God's plans. God spelt out what he wanted Moses to do. Why was Moses so reluctant to obey?

But if you are unwilling to serve the LORD, then choose today whom you will serve. Would you prefer the gods your ancestors served beyond the Euphrates? Or will it be the gods of the Amorites in whose land you now live? But as for me and my family, we will serve the LORD.

Joshua 24:15

Q: Whom do you serve?

2 TAKE CARE

Read

Numbers 20:1–12

Moses had been an obedient servant of God for many years but could still get it wrong. Maybe all the moaning had put him in a bad mood. Maybe he wanted an opportunity to reassert his God-given authority over Israel. Maybe he thought God wouldn't notice if he didn't quite follow his plan exactly. Whatever his motives, Moses didn't do what God wanted.

Q: Why do you think God punished him so harshly?

Q: Moses knew God better than anyone. He'd even spoken to him face to face, 'as a man speaks to his friend' (Exodus 33:11). Why do you think he disobeyed God here?

Q: Even great men of faith like Moses could still get it wrong sometimes. His example reminds us that we shouldn't drop our guard. Paul says, 'If you think you are standing strong, be careful, for you, too, may fall into the same sin' (1 Corinthians 10:12). How can we reduce our chances of falling into the same trap as Moses?

'For every child of God defeats this evil world by trusting Christ to give the victory' (1 John 5:4). Give thanks that Jesus' death on the cross means that our sin can be forgiven rather than separating us from God for ever.

3 LOVE IS THE KEY

Are you good at keeping rules? Do you drive the right way round car parks? Cheat in board games? Declare everything to the taxman? Does it matter?

Sometimes people see God as the King of Rules, just waiting for a chance to punish anyone who breaks them. However, the Bible makes it clear that what God really wants is to have a relationship with us that is built on love.

Read

Matthew 22:36–40 and 1 John 2:5

Jesus sums up our whole purpose in two commandments, loving God wholeheartedly and loving one another. Our relationship with God is not built on rules but on love; his love for us and our love for him and his people. Get that right and everything else, including our lifestyle, falls into place. Obviously obedience still matters; John reminds us that it's easy to say we love God and his people, but it's the way we live that shows whether our love is really true or not.

Q: 'You must love the Lord your God with all your heart, all your soul, and all your mind,' says Jesus (Matthew 22:37). What does it mean to keep our relationship with God at the centre of our lives?

Q: Loving one another doesn't just mean being nice to people we like, or even just other Christians. Who do you find it difficult to love? How could you show God's love to someone like this? Who could you show God's love to today?

2 At the crossroads

Our temptations. Are they one too many sticky cakes or changing a figure on our tax return? Passing off our colleague's work as our own or blaming a friend for a row of our making? Whatever our weaknesses, does it really matter if we give in?

Maybe we don't need to beat ourselves up over every tiny slip, but we can't ignore our failures completely. Many lives are marred in some way by the inability to resist temptation. Perhaps it's watching or reading something better avoided, maybe pushing others aside to gain power and status, or giving in, yet again, to the witty, but hurtful, reply. Is it just the way we're made, something we have to live with, or is it possible to find the power to change?

Here we see Jesus facing his own time of temptation. Unlike us, he never gives in, and in his resistance we can see ways of facing our next challenge with renewed and strengthened defences.

Setting Out

Q: Do you think our society believes in a real being called Satan or the devil?

Q: Whether people believe in him or not, most would have an image of what he looks like. How do you think they would describe him?

Q: Where would they get these ideas about his appearance?

Q: If everything you knew about the devil came from the media: films, TV, adverts etc, what would you think his character was like?

Q: Why do you think society represents the devil in this way?

Q: Do you think they are right to do so? Why?

Signposts

Q: The Bible takes Satan very seriously; he is never dismissed as a figment of the imagination, a figure of fun or 'naughty but nice'. What do these verses say Satan is really like?

John 8:44
Ephesians 2:2
1 Peter 5:8

Q: What does he want to do?

John 10:10
1 Thessalonians 3:5

Read

Matthew 4:1–11

Israel had once been tested for 40 years in the desert.

Q: Why did God put them to the test? (Deuteronomy 8:2)

Many hundreds of years later, Jesus faces 40 days of testing.

Q: Why do you think he was tested for 40 days rather than any other length of time?

Q: What was the point of putting Jesus to the test? (Psalm 26:2,3)

Q: Would it really have mattered if Jesus had succumbed to Satan's pressure? Surely God would have forgiven him, wouldn't he? (2 Corinthians 5:21 and 1 John 1:9; 3:5)

THE THREE TEMPTATIONS (Matthew 4:3–10)

Read

1 John 2:15–17

Loving God or loving the world will result in very different attitudes to life.

Q: What shows that someone has chosen to live the world's way?

Q: What bad news does John have for those who have made this choice?

Q: In the wilderness, Jesus' priorities are put to the test. When things get tough, will he really choose to live God's way or will he go the world's way instead?

Q: In which ways is Jesus being tempted to misuse his powers?

Q: How might this be a temptation for us too?

Q: How did Jesus resist?

Q: In the second test (4:5,6) Satan quotes scripture (Psalm 91:11,12) to Jesus. Why do you think Jesus didn't listen to him?

Q: Both Jesus and Satan used scripture to support their arguments. When we do the same, how can we know we're using it correctly?

Eventually Jesus' resistance led to Satan leaving (for now). Luke says, 'When the Devil had finished tempting Jesus, he left him *until the next opportunity came*' (Luke 4:13, italics added). Temptation is always lurking, so we need to be prepared for it.

THREE WAYS TO STRENGTHEN OUR DEFENCES

1 Know God's Word

Jesus relied on the same defence each time – his knowledge of the Word of God. Psalm 119:11 says, 'I have hidden your word in my heart, that I might not sin against you.'

Q: What does it mean to hide God's Word in our heart? How might this help us to avoid sin?

Q: Satan was very familiar with God's Word but it didn't stop him sinning. Why was that?

Q: Which book of the Bible do you most enjoy reading? Why?

Q: Are there parts of the Bible that you've never or rarely looked at? Does it matter?

Q: What would help you to read these parts of the Bible more often?

Q: Knowing what God's Word says doesn't mean we necessarily live as God wants. How can God's Word help us to live God's way?

2 Know our weaknesses

Spiritual highs and lows

Q: Jesus went out into the wilderness immediately after the spiritual high point of his baptism. Have you experienced similar high points in your life? Did you find they were followed by particularly difficult times or not?

Q: Why might such high points in our lives leave us vulnerable to difficult times afterwards?

Q: How can we prepare ourselves to cope with such ups and downs in life?

Personal weak points

Jesus was hungry, a point of physical weakness that Satan could work on. Strong emotions can be another weak point. Paul says, 'for anger gives a mighty foothold to the Devil' (Ephesians 4:27).

Q: How might a powerful emotion such as anger give a foothold to the devil?

Q: What other emotions or physical states might make someone vulnerable to temptation?

Q: What about you? Which of these is most likely to affect you?

Q: Not all these emotions and states are sinful in themselves. How can we reduce the risk of falling into sin in these situations?

3 Know when to stand firm and when to run

Read

1 Timothy 6:11; 2 Timothy 2:22 and James 4:7

Jesus went to face Satan's testing, not because he fancied a challenge but because it was important. Sometimes the wise thing is to avoid situations where we'll face temptation and run away instead.

Q: What kind of situations should we run away from? What does it mean to do that?

Q: Why do you think people sometimes find it hard to run away from temptation?

Q: Sometimes we are tempted to sin through persecution and hardship. What should we do then, stand firm or run away? Why?

Q: What about you? Where should you be standing firm? Or running away?

Finally

Q: In the desert, Jesus had to choose whether to go God's way or not. What do you think led him to make the choice to obey God?

Q: What could we do that would help us make that same choice?

Prayer

The choices that Jesus made had eternal consequences.

Begin by reading these verses from Hebrews:

Because God's children are human beings—made of flesh and blood—Jesus also became flesh and blood by being born in human form. For only as a human being could he die, and only by dying could he break the power of the Devil, who had the power of death. Only in this way could he deliver those who have lived all their lives as slaves to the fear of dying.

Hebrews 2:14,15

Then pray together, aloud or in silence as you prefer, giving thanks for Jesus:
For resisting the temptation to do things the world's way instead of God's way;
For choosing to die for us and bearing the consequences of our sin;
For his resurrection, ending Satan's power over death and over us as God's people.

Groups may also want to give people an opportunity to share situations where they are struggling to stand up to, or run away from, temptation. Pray for one another. Is there some practical support you could give to those facing such situations?

En Route

Memorising Scripture

You might like to try committing verses or short passages from the Bible to memory. If so, choose one verse to learn for each remaining session of the series. Remember to learn both the verse and its Bible reference; you want to know where it comes from.

Groups could all learn the same verse(s), perhaps awarding a prize to everyone who can recite them all correctly at the end of the series.

What to learn

Many Bibles have topical lists of helpful verses you could select from.

The Navigators publish two versions of their Topical Memory System (Navpress) which include cards with memory verses printed on them.

Use a verse that stands out from the session, so this time, for example, perhaps use either Psalm 119:11 or 1 Timothy 6:11.

Further Afield

1 A SLIPPERY SLOPE

Read

2 Samuel 11:1–4

David makes a series of wrong choices that lead him deeper and deeper into sin.

Q: What wrong choices did he make?

Q: How could David have chosen differently at each point and so avoided further sin?

Q: With every wrong choice, it gets harder to get back on the right path. Obviously the best plan is to make the right choices in the first place. Can you remember times in your own life when a series of wrong choices took you deeper into sin?

Pray that you would have the wisdom and the courage to make God's choices every time.

2 CONSEQUENCES

Read

2 Samuel 11:5–27

Once Bathsheba went home, David must have believed that his sin was both hidden and past. Unfortunately for him, the consequences of his sin were about to become very public.

Q: Why did David want to hide the truth about Bathsheba's pregnancy?

Q: Who did he hurt as a result?

Q: How was David's relationship with God affected by this episode?

Even when our sin remains hidden it still harms us and our relationship with God. Think about the wrong things you've done that have caused harm to you, others and your relationship with God. Pray for God's forgiveness and ask him to show you if there is something you could do to start putting things right.

3 REBUKE

Read

2 Samuel 12

Q: How do you react when someone tells you (tactfully or not) that you've done something wrong?

Q: What gave Nathan the authority to point out David's sin to him?

Q: When would it be wrong for us to point out another person's sin? When is it right?

Q: Nathan approached David with a story rather than spelling out his sin directly. What might we learn from that tactic?

Pray that you would be willing to hear the truth about your sins from anyone, whoever they are and however they do it!

3 The hardest choice

Are you a morning person, one who loves leaping out of bed as dawn breaks to iron, wash the car and go for a run, all before going to work? No? Are you a night owl, the one who likes to watch films that start after midnight and who loves to dance the night away? Times of getting up, going to bed and all the choices in between can be a struggle between what we know we should do and what we'd like to do. We'd like to lie in bed but church is calling. We'd like to hit the chip shop for lunch but our cholesterol count is rising. We'd like to go out and party but our best friend is lying bored in a hospital bed. In the midst of our own preferences, there's also another factor. What does God want us to do?

In this study we've travelled forward from Jesus facing temptation to another test in Gethsemane. Now he has to choose. Will he take the path that he'd prefer or put his own desires aside to do what God wants? As we see him make the choice to go God's way, we find help to make that same choice too.

Setting Out

Whether we're touchy-feely or level-headed, easygoing or emotional, feelings make a difference to the day. Get up feeling happy or excited and the day is likely to be very different from one you begin feeling drained and sad. Face a choice where one route brings happiness and the other doesn't and most people would choose the first every time.

How much do your feelings affect your choices? For each pair of questions, choose which of A or B is most like you.

Are you more likely to:

A Travel to a new destination with your route meticulously planned in advance and your map open at the right page throughout?

B Travel to a new destination trusting to your innate sense of direction to get you there?

A Buy a new house because it meets everything on the list of requirements you've made in advance?

B Buy a new house because it feels right when you walk in?

A Accept a job offer because the job has good prospects and offers the right conditions?

B Accept a job offer because people were so friendly and the office looked nice?

A Buy a pet after you've listed the pros and cons, asked friends and made all the preparations first?

B Buy a pet because you've seen a cute one (or two) in the pet shop?

A Plan menus for each day's tea at the beginning of the week and stick to them?

B See how you feel each evening and then see whether you need to go shopping or not?

Add up your As and Bs. Which did you have most of?

Mostly As might suggest you make decisions after careful planning, weighing up the pros and cons.

Mostly Bs might suggest that you're inclined to make decisions on impulse and on the way you feel at the time.

Is that fair?

Q: Think of real-life decisions you have made. Which way did you make them? Did it work out well?

Q: What do you think are the advantages of these different approaches to decision making?

Signposts

Read

Matthew 26:36–46

Q: What words would sum up Jesus' emotional state in the Garden of Gethsemane?

Q: What would you do if someone you love was faced with doing something that terrified them and you could get them out of it? Why?

Q: God had the power to save Jesus, his beloved Son, from the cross. Do you think he wanted to do that? Why do you think he didn't?

Q: Jesus would have preferred not to go to the cross and he could have chosen not to. What made him decide to go through with it?

DOESN'T GOD WANT ME TO BE HAPPY?

Feelings can be great; life would be very boring without them, wouldn't it? However, sometimes we listen to our feelings even when they'll lead us into unwise choices – 'If it feels good, do it' – and we can all fall into this trap. Have you ever explained a choice by saying 'God wants me to be happy', or heard someone else doing so? If we act on this (and the Bible never says this is what God wants most for us), we make choices based on our feelings of the moment, not on what God really wants for us. Of course God doesn't take pleasure in seeing us suffering and unhappy, but his first priority for us is that we live his way.

Peter says, 'Obey God because you are his children. Don't slip back into your old ways of doing evil; you didn't know any better then. But now you must be holy in everything you do, just as God—who chose you to be his children—is holy. For he himself has said, "You must be holy because I am holy"' (1 Peter 1:14–16). True happiness is found not in always following our feelings, which change from moment to moment, but in following God's plans for us. Psalm 119:35 says, 'Make me walk along the path of your commands, for that is where my happiness is found.'

If Jesus had followed his human feelings in Gethsemane he would never have gone to the cross. Instead he put them aside and chose short-term suffering for the sake of his eternal happiness – the choice God wanted him to make.

Four things helped Jesus choose the path of true and lasting happiness in Gethsemane:

1 Prayer

'Sit here, while I go on ahead to pray' Matthew 26:36.

Q: All through his ministry, Jesus made time to be alone with God; he opened every moment of his life to God's involvement. How do you think Jesus' prayers allowed God to help him in Gethsemane?

Q: How much of a priority is prayer in your life?

Q: Think back over the last year. Has prayer become more important to you or not? Why?

Q: How could more time alone with God make a difference to your daily life? How will you achieve this?

2 Prior planning

'I want your will, not mine' Matthew 26:39.

Read

John 6:38

Q: Long before the emotional turmoil of Gethsemane, Jesus had made the decision that he would obey God. How did making this decision in advance help him to choose God's way in Gethsemane?

Q: When might we face situations where making a decision in advance to obey God would help us do his will?

Q: Are you facing a choice where what you'd like to do doesn't match what God wants you to do?

Q: How could you find the strength to follow God's path?

If you meet as a group, how could you support one another?

3 Knowing his purpose

'The time has come' Matthew 26:45.

Read

Matthew 20:28

Jesus knew why he had come to earth (1 Timothy 1:15).

Q: How did this sense of purpose help him to make his choice in Gethsemane?

Read

1 Peter 2:9,10

Q: It wasn't just Jesus that had a clear purpose for his time on earth; God has just as clear a purpose for us all. How can knowing that purpose help us to obey him too?

4 The prize

Read

Hebrews 12:1,2 and 1 Corinthians 9:24,25

Q: In Gethsemane, Jesus didn't make his choice on the basis of what would happen in the next few hours but by focusing on the eternal consequences. Our choices also affect more than our life on earth. How might our choices today have an eternal impact?

Q: What prize did Jesus win through his obedience?

Q: What about us? What prize are we running to win?

Finally

In Gethsemane, Jesus faced a tough choice. Like him, we too can find making choices tough. Even when they're made life doesn't necessarily get easier; right choices can bring tough consequences.

Q: When might a right choice bring difficult long-term consequences, perhaps at work, in relationships or in using money?

Q: What kind of support could we offer people in these situations?

Q: Why is it important to encourage people who suffer for making a right choice?

Q: Are there people you know, perhaps members of your group, who are suffering for choosing God's way? How can you support them?

Prayer

Pray for any of the issues raised in this session, particularly for anyone in your group who needs help to make a right choice or to live with the consequences of one.

To finish, have someone read the following reflection, ending with a short time of silence.

No greater love

I force myself away.
Soothing sounds of friendly voices fade
and cloaked by evening dark
I am alone.

Terror grabs its opportunity,
leaking into every thought.
I'm sobbing, pleading, longing for release,
but no such promise comes.

I didn't hear his voice at first,
too much noise inside.
Quietening I find I know the words before they come again.
Trust me.

I make the choice.
Fear raging on,
clinging to this hope,
I stand up,
step forward.
My hour has come.

Further Afield

1 FINDING MEANING

Read

Ecclesiastes 2:1–11

Q: Where did the writer look for meaning in life?

Q: Is it wrong to do these things?

Q: Why didn't they bring him a lasting sense of meaning?

Q: The writer sought meaning and happiness in life in the things God created, rather than in God himself. What are you most likely to replace God with?

Pray that God would help you to seek meaning and happiness in your relationship with him rather than in his gifts.

2 LIVING THE LIFE

Read

Philippians 3:4–14

Q: What did Paul once think 'so very important'? (v 7)

Q: What has he replaced these things with? (vs 8,9)

Q: Has he given up on obedient living? (vs 12–14)

How we live shows whether Jesus is really Lord of our lives and Paul hasn't stopped working towards the day when his life will truly show that. Paul also reminds us that our first priority in life is a vital and living relationship with Jesus, and our obedience flows from that as a response to the One who brings us life.

Spend some extra time, now if you can, or make a date with your diary, to nurture your relationship with Jesus. Perhaps you could use the opportunity to try something a bit different, perhaps spending time in silence, meditating on a verse or listening to music, as well as time in prayer.

3 RUNNING TO WIN

Read

1 Corinthians 9:24,25 and 2 Timothy 4:6–8

Q: Are you, or were you once, any good at running races? Did you ever win any prizes?

Some will have happy memories of winning prizes, others of trying to avoid running anywhere, of trailing in last, or even being good but never quite good enough to win. Whatever our past experiences, we are now involved in a race that we can win, with a prize that will last for ever.

Q: Paul says, 'You also must run in such a way that you will win.' How can we run this race to be sure of winning?

Q: And what is this 'crown of righteousness' we can win? (See also James 1:12.)

Q: Do you need to sharpen up the way you are running this race? How could you do that?

Pray that God will help you to keep on running with the finishing line in mind.

4 Truth and justice

'It's not fair!' Do you remember that cry from childhood? Stand in any playground, wait a few minutes, and you'll be sure to hear it. A sense of justice doesn't wear off as we hit adulthood, though, does it? We're still quick to notice injustice in our own lives, even if we don't always grab or punch or scream in response. How should we respond to injustice in our own lives? What about the lives of others? Are we as quick to see others' suffering and to get involved and do something about it? What about the times it's our lifestyle that causes that injustice? Do we care? Do we even notice?

In this study, we see Jesus facing the injustice of his trial. What does his response show us about dealing with injustice in the 21st Century? How does God really feel about the injustice in our world, and what does that mean for the way we live our lives?

Setting Out

'It's not fair!'

For each of these situations, imagine how you would feel if they happened to you.

1 You've queued in the Post Office for 30 minutes when someone walks in, goes straight to the front of the queue and is served immediately.

2 Your employer gives everyone a Christmas bonus. You've all worked for the same length of time and are all on the same pay scale but your colleagues are all given twice as much as you.

3 You've gone out for the evening and bump into an acquaintance who then gets embroiled in an argument with someone else. You all end up being thrown out.

Q: Do you think these situations are unfair to you?

Q: If so, do you think someone should put things right or should you just forget about it? Why?

Q: What if you had been present when these things happened to someone else?

What would you personally have done about it? Something or nothing?
Why?

Q: In the face of injustice, do you think you are more likely to put up with it
or to be crusading and angry? Does it matter?

Signposts

Read /   ✓
Matthew 26:57–68 and Matthew 27:11–26

1 THE PROSECUTION CASE

Matthew describes the reactions of Caiaphas and the Sanhedrin, Pilate and the
ordinary people to Jesus after his arrest. For each of these consider:

γ • How would you have expected them to react to Jesus?
γ • In reality, how did they react to him?
⤫ • Why do you think they responded as they did?

If you are meeting with a group you might like to divide up into two
smaller groups, the first looking at the behaviour of Caiaphas, the Sanhedrin
and the ordinary people in the Matthew 26 reading, the second at the behaviour
of Pilate and the ordinary people in the Matthew 27 reading. Allow a few
minutes to discuss your ideas, then report back to the other group.

Jesus found all these people ranged against him. However, in the face of such
trouble, we would surely expect his friends and disciples to be there supporting
him.

Q: How did they react to Jesus' arrest? (You can read about Peter in Matthew
26:57,58 and 69–75, Judas in 26:47–50 and 27:3–10, and the other
disciples in Matthew 26:35,56.)

Q: Why did they react like this?

✗ Q: Many of the hostile reactions to Jesus grew out of fear. What were people afraid of?

Even today people still fear those who are different.

Q: Where is this happening in the world?

Q: Where is this happening in your local community?

Q: Have you ever found yourself reacting in this way? Or been on the receiving end? Why was that?

Q: What sort of things could we do to help reduce or even overcome such fears?

2 THE DEFENCE

The reactions to Jesus may seem surprising, but perhaps Jesus' behaviour is even more unexpected.

Q: Imagine you're on the receiving end of a false accusation. Maybe you've been in a situation like this at work, in school, even in the courts themselves. How would you/did you feel in this situation?

Q: When given the opportunity to respond in such a situation, would you think it wise to remain silent? Why?

< Q: At times during his trial Jesus speaks, but at other times he chooses to remain silent. Why do you think he doesn't take the opportunity to defend himself against false accusations? (Matthew 26:60–63a and 27:12–14)

✗ Q: What's so different about the questions he does reply to? (Matthew 26:63,64 and 27:11)

3 THE VERDICT

Jesus was found guilty and sentenced to death. As the Son of God he could have walked away or called down angels to rescue him at any moment (Matthew 26:53), but he didn't.

Read

Ephesians 1:7 and 1 Peter 2:24; 3:18

Q: Why did he allow this injustice to take place?

Q: The actions of the Jewish authorities and Pilate's weakness saw Jesus sent to the cross, but who truly bears the ultimate responsibility for Jesus' death? Why do you say that?

4 OUR RESPONSE TO INJUSTICE

Jesus accepted the injustice of his trial, but that doesn't mean justice isn't important.

Read

2 Chronicles 19:7; Proverbs 31:8,9; Revelation 6:9–11

Q: How does God view injustice?

Q: What kind of injustices do we see in society today?

Q: What sorts of things could we do about them?

Q: Jesus refused to defend himself in the face of injustice. Should we ever do the same? (You might find it helpful to read Paul's comments in 1 Corinthians 6:1–8 and Jesus' words in Matthew 5:38–42.)

Q: How can we know when it's right to attack injustice and when to submit to it?

Prayer

Make a list of some of the people and situations currently experiencing injustice:

1 in your local community
2 in your country
3 in the wider world

You might find it helpful to look through copies of recent national and local newspapers for ideas.

Choose one or two situations for each section and pray for them over the next few weeks.

Groups might like to ask individuals to keep abreast of these situations so they can update the group at subsequent meetings.

There may also be those within the group who are experiencing injustice in some form at the moment. If so, give them the opportunity to share that with the group, even if they prefer not to go into details. Is there some way the group can support them?

Pray together, aloud or silently, for these situations.

En Route

As an individual, or as a group, consider doing something practical to highlight and oppose injustice in the world.

For example:

1 Protest on behalf of those unjustly imprisoned or suffering other abuses of their human rights.
   Advice is available from both Christian organisations such as Open Doors (www.opendoorsuk.org), and Release International (www.releaseinterna-tional.org), and also from Amnesty (www.amnesty.org.uk).

2 By buying Fairtrade products such as tea and coffee which guarantee the pro-ducers a fair wage for their work. Maybe groups could use fairly traded tea and coffee for the remainder of their meetings, if they don't do so already.

How else could you oppose injustice in the world today?

1 with others, as a group, a church or a group of churches
2 by yourself

Further Afield

1 DEALING WITH INJUSTICE

Read

Genesis 39

Q: Joseph received a punishment he certainly didn't deserve. How would you have felt in his situation?

Q: With Joseph in charge, Potiphar found that his household and his business affairs flourished. Why then did he treat Joseph so unjustly?

Q: When life is so unfair to us it's easy to believe that God has abandoned us. Why might someone feel that way? Do you think Joseph felt like that? How do you think he coped with his emotions?

Q: What can we learn from Joseph's experiences that might help us when we face injustice ourselves?

2 LOVE YOUR ENEMIES

Read

Matthew 5:44 and Luke 6:35

Q: How do these verses say we should respond to those that harm us?

Q: Think back to a time when someone has hurt you in some way. How did you feel about them? Was loving forgiveness top of your agenda or not? Why was that?

Q: Jesus gives practical examples of what he means by loving our enemies; we should pray for them, do good to them and be generous to them. Why does he want us to behave like this?

Q: Has anyone come to mind as you thought about these questions? How could you show God's love to them?

Q: Feelings of hurt and anger can mean that love is the last thing we want to show to someone who has caused us harm. Does that ring true for you or for someone you know? How could we pray for ourselves, or those we know, in such a situation?

Q: Sometimes the harm caused, perhaps through abuse, is so great and ongoing that any contact would be unwise and dangerous. Is it possible to remain safe and still show love towards someone like this? Should we even try?

3 MORE THAN SAYING SORRY

Read

Luke 19:1–10 and Leviticus 6:1–7

Zacchaeus had caused harm to others through his dubious tax-collecting practices. (As chief tax inspector he farmed out the responsibility to collect tax to others, taking a large cut for himself.)

Q: How did he respond when he met Jesus?

Q: Why was it important that Zacchaeus did more than say sorry, but also did something practical to put things right?

Q: Whether we are corrupt like Zacchaeus, or see ourselves as generally law-abiding, we too sometimes have to put things right in a practical way to make restitution to someone. Can you think of an example of a situation where this would be appropriate?

Q: Is there someone in your life that this applies to?

Ask God to show you how you could make restitution to anyone you have harmed.

5 Hope in the darkness

*H*ave you ever chosen to spend the night out of doors, or do you like the comfort of a mattress and sheets too much to even consider it? It is said that the darkest hour is just before the dawn; that when the darkness seems to be completely impenetrable that's really the moment when the first streaks of dawn light appear in the sky.

In this session we come to the moment in history when it seemed that this time the dawn would not appear, that the darkness had really won at last. For a short time, the death of Jesus appeared to be the end, the victory going to the powers of darkness, the Son of God defeated. With hindsight we know that wasn't so, but even here, as we focus on Good Friday, we can see glimmers of hope, reminders that in the darkest moments of our lives the light of God's power and love still shines on.

Setting Out

Optimist or pessimist – is your glass half-full or half-empty?

How would you respond in these situations?

1 The nightmare comes true. The exam's today and you've forgotten to do any preparation. Do you:

    a Stay in bed. You've no chance of passing so why bother turning up?

    b Leap out of bed and give it a go. What have you got to lose?

    c Something else?

2 You enter a competition to win tickets for something you'd really like to see. Do you:

    a Make a hotel booking as soon as you've posted the entry. How can you lose?

    b Buy your own tickets? You'll never win.

    c Something else?

3 You're walking towards the supermarket tills and all the queues are long. Do you:

    a Check exactly how much people have in their trolleys so you can choose the quickest queue?

    b Take the first queue you come to? It won't make any difference, you always get it wrong.

    c Something else?

4 You look out of the window. The sky is grey and the ground is damp but there's a tiny patch of blue directly above you. Do you:

    a Put on your raincoat and wellies and grab your umbrella? It's just the calm before the storm.

    b Put away your umbrella and make sure you've got your sunglasses handy? It's brightening up.

    c Something else?

Q: What do you think are the advantages of approaching life as an optimist? And a pessimist?

Q: Are there downsides to these approaches too? If so, what?

Q: Which are you most likely to be? Why do you think that is?

Signposts

Read

Matthew 20:17–19 and John 12:32–34

Q: How did the disciples and the crowd respond to the news that Jesus was going to die?

Q: Why do you think they didn't believe or understand him?

Q: Would it have made a difference if they had taken his message in? If so, how?

Even for the most naturally upbeat optimists among the disciples, it must surely have been impossible to foresee anything good coming from the events of Good Friday. As you read the following verses try to imagine what it was like for the disciples to live through that day without understanding what was going to happen next.

Read
Matthew 27:32–50

THREE MESSAGES OF HOPE

1 It's never too late

Q: How did people respond when they saw Jesus, who'd claimed to be the Son of God, dying on the cross (vs 39–43)?

Q: Why do you think they reacted like this?

Read
Matthew 27:44 and Luke 23:39–43

Q: Even the criminals mocked Jesus. What do you think made one of them later change sides?

That criminal made the decision to trust Jesus very late in life!

Q: Imagine two people. One makes that same decision early in life and follows Jesus, possibly even suffering for doing so, for many years. The other makes it just days before their death but receives the same forgiveness and promise of eternal life. Some might feel that this is unfair. Do you?

Q: Why do you think God allows this to happen? (You might find Romans 5:8 and Ephesians 2:8 helpful.)

Q: Imagine someone else then said, 'Well if that's the case I'll eat, drink and be merry and then repent (much) later on in life.' Maybe you hold that view yourself or know someone who does. What makes it worth following Jesus now instead of waiting?

Q: Have you made the decision to follow Jesus? If so, why did you decide to take the plunge when you did? If not, what is stopping you?

2 God never abandons us

Less than 24 hours after the Last Supper, Jesus was dead.

Q: How do you think the disciples felt about the three years they'd just spent following Jesus?

Q: How about the future? How do you think they felt about that?

Q: How can we be sure that, despite appearances, God was still in control of events here?

Q: In this darkest of moments, it must have seemed to the disciples as though everything was over, their dreams and hopes had been permanently shattered. We too can face times when it seems that we have been wasting our time following Jesus, that he has abandoned us. Have you ever felt like that?

Q: If so, and if that experience is now in the past, what brought you through it?

Q: What does the Bible promise us in times of disappointment and darkness? Read Isaiah 43:1,2 and Jeremiah 29:11.

Q: How could the experiences of the disciples here encourage us when we face tough situations?

3 Death is not the end

Read
Psalm 22:1–18 and Matthew 27:46

As Jesus took on the sins of the world on the cross, he experienced something that was even worse than the physical suffering – rejection by God. He cries out with words from Psalm 22:1: 'My God, my God, why have you forsaken me?'

Q: Many Psalms describe feelings of separation from God. Why do you think Jesus chose to quote from this one in particular?

Read

Psalm 22:19–31

Q: The suffering and separation described in the Psalm aren't all it has to say. What do these verses from the end of the Psalm promise God's people?

At the darkest hour of Jesus' life he quotes from a Psalm that points to God's promises for the future, to the hope that lies beyond suffering and death.

Prayer

Groups should begin by choosing someone to read the Bible passages. After each one, everyone may read the response together then pray in silence, using the suggestions.

Reader: 'In the beginning the Word already existed. He was with God, and he was God. He was in the beginning with God. He created everything there is. Nothing exists that he didn't make. Life itself was in him, and this life gives light to everyone. The light shines through the darkness, and the darkness can never extinguish it.'

John 1:1–5.

Response: Lord, you are the Creator God, the source of all life.

Think about the last few days. Where have you seen or experienced God's creation in that time? What do these things show you about God's character, what he is like? Praise him for these things.

Reader: 'But he was wounded and crushed for our sins. He was beaten that we might have peace. He was whipped, and we were healed!' Isaiah 53:5.

Response: Lord, you are the Sinless One, who chose to bear the punishment for our sin.

Again reflect on the last few days. What have you done that was wrong? Perhaps it was a one-off, a weak moment. Perhaps it's part of a pattern and you keep on making the same wrong choice. Remember that those things sent Jesus to the cross for you. Ask God to forgive you and give you a new start. Reflect on what you could do to make amends for your actions.

Reader: 'That is why we have a great High Priest who has gone to heaven, Jesus the Son of God. Let us cling to him and never stop trusting him. This High Priest of ours understands our weaknesses, for he faced all the same temptations we do, yet he did not sin. So let us come boldly to the throne of our gracious God. There we will receive his mercy, and we will find grace to help us when we need it.' Hebrews 4:14–16.

Response: Lord, you are the Servant King, the one who truly understands what it is like to be me.

As a man, Jesus knew what it was like to suffer; he experienced hunger, pain and injustice. He knew grief and fear, betrayal and death.

Think about yourself and those you love. Who is suffering or facing trouble at the moment?

What help do they need?

Pray for them, especially that they will experience the presence and the love of Jesus, the one who understands. Consider whether you could offer them any other support.

Further Afield

1 A KING'S WELCOME

Read

Philippians 2:1–11

Q: If you knew God's Son was about to arrive on earth, what kind of welcome would you expect him to receive?

Q: Why did Jesus give up the right to such a welcome?

Q: Are there times when we should give up our rightful expectations for the benefit of others? What might that mean for you at home; at work; at church?

2 OUR RESPONSE

Read

Psalm 19:14 and Matthew 16:24,25

The cross should change the way we live.

Q: What kind of life should a follower of Jesus be leading? Why?

Q: What are you finding most difficult to get right at the moment: words, thoughts or deeds? Why is that?

Q: What could you do to start the process of change in that area? Do you need to ask someone else for help or support?

Pray that God would help you to live your life in a way he considers worthy. Spend some time in silence, and allow him to point out where things are going well and not so well at the moment.

3 A RESPONSE OF PRAISE

Read

Psalm 145

Q: In praise, we celebrate God's character. What aspects of God's character does the writer describe in this Psalm?

'My mouth will speak in praise of the Lord' (v 21, NIV).

Whatever your composing skills, however long or short you want it to be, write your own psalm of praise to God. End by praying through that psalm.

6 A new beginning

*H*ave you ever fancied going back in time and having another go at parts of your life? Maybe sometimes you just want to rerun a conversation that didn't go as you'd hoped. Maybe sometimes it's more fundamental than that; you want another chance at that big decision, another opportunity to get life right. It's never going to happen though, is it? We have to get it right first time or put up with the consequences. As a result, self-help books abound on shop shelves, offering ways to transform the person you've become: *Fifty ways to create a new you; Ten steps to a happier life; How to fulfil your potential.*

But do they work? Isn't it more likely that even if some find a short-term benefit, in the end they too will find that motivation wanes, stresses build up, and the 'new me', the 'happier life' and 'fulfilled potential' get shelved. Here, in our final study, we see that the resurrection brought good news. Instead of struggling, and failing, to sort ourselves out on our own, the power of Jesus allows us to begin again, to have a new life and the chance to become the person God made us to be.

Setting Out

Sometimes crime stories feature suspects or witnesses with a phenomenal recall of their actions days, weeks or months earlier, often without a diary or anything else as a reminder.

✓ Q: Do you think that's realistic? Why, or why not?

✓ Q: Think back to last Saturday. What can you remember about it? For example, do you remember what you had for lunch, what the weather was like or what was in the news headlines?

Q: What about a month ago today? Or this time last year?

Q: Maybe you're an exception, but why do you think people can find such questions difficult to answer?

Q: Some events do stay in the memory of course: Hiroshima, the assassination of JFK, the fall of the Berlin Wall, 9/11… it is said that people remember where they were when such events happened. Do you remember where you were and how you heard about 9/11, the most recent of these? What about the others?

✓Q: Are there other news events, significant or not quite so significant, that bring back memories of what you were doing at the time?

✓Q: Why do you think these things stand out in our memories for decades afterwards, when the details of our daily lives can be quickly forgotten?

Signposts

On the third day after the death of Jesus, his followers experience a truly significant event, one they could never forget – the unique return to life of a dead man.

Read
Matthew 28:1–20

THE POWER OF THE RESURRECTION

Like some other historical events, the resurrection was more than a stunning one-off moment; its effects reverberate throughout history. Uniquely, the resurrection also makes an impact beyond history, in eternity.

1 It can change us for ever

Read
2 Corinthians 5:17 and Colossians 3:9,10

Q: Some people can look back on a time when they definitely weren't a Christian but, equally definitely, are now. If that's true for you, do you think that you are 'different' now that you are a Christian? If so, how?

Over the centuries Israel ably demonstrated that people cannot live truly obedient lives; they will always fall back into sin, 'but now…', as Paul says (Ephesians 2:13), after the resurrection everything is different.

✓ Q: What does Paul describe as new?

✓ Q: What would you hope that such a new person would be like?

✓ Q: Unfortunately Christian lifestyles can seem almost identical to those of non-Christians. Why do you think that happens?

✓ Q: So we are new people who still fall into sin. That doesn't sound very different from before! What is it that the resurrection changed for ever? (See Romans 4:23–25.)

Q: In our struggle against sin, what reassurance can this verse offer us?

2 Everything will have a new start

Read

Romans 8:19–21; 2 Peter 3:13; Revelation 21:1–5

It's not just us, God's people, that are changed. One day everything will start again.

✓ Q: Why does God want to create a new heaven and a new earth?

✓ Q: How will they be different from the ones we have now?

3 Death's power is broken

Read Hebrews 2:14,15; 2 Timothy 1:8–10

✓ Q: Death isn't something we generally like to think about much. What is it about death that frightens many people?

✓ Q: How might such a fear affect the way they live their life?

Q: Of course, until Jesus returns, we are still going to die. How then does his death and resurrection free us from that fear of death?

Read

1 Corinthians 15:50–57 and 2 Corinthians 5:1–5

✓ Q: What's the last object you replaced because it didn't work properly anymore?

✓ Q: If you could replace bits of your body in the same way, what would you most like to renew?

Q: Paul's description of a transformed body is good news, isn't it? Why do you think Paul puts so much emphasis on the promise of a physical resurrection, a real bodily life after death?

✓ Q: If fear of dying can affect the whole of life, a hope in life beyond death can affect it too. How do you think such a hope should alter the way we live our lives on earth?

Q: Do you think it has done that for you? Why, or why not?

LOOKING FORWARD

Read

Luke 12:15–34

Many people believe that this life is all there is; once you die that's it. The resurrection showed us that, on the contrary, this life, whilst precious in itself, is also preparation for life beyond death.

✓ Q: What does Jesus say our priorities in life should be? Why?

✓ Q: If you don't believe in life after death then obviously Jesus' priorities don't make sense. What priorities might you have in life then?

As citizens of earth, we are under pressure to accept the world's priorities and it's easy to do that rather than focusing on the things Jesus says are truly important. We're not just citizens of earth though, we are also citizens of heaven (Philippians 3:20) and so we are called to live differently.

Q: What does your lifestyle suggest are your true priorities?

Do you make the effort to build worldly security or eternal security?
What do you spend your time and money on?
Who do you spend them with?

Q: What else in our lives might show what we really consider important?

Q: Is there some way your priorities, and therefore your lifestyle, need to change? If so, what first step could you take towards bringing that about?

If you are meeting with a group perhaps you could share that step with the rest of the group so that they can pray for you and encourage you through the process of change.

Finally

Jesus left his disciples with these words:

Therefore, go and make disciples of all the nations, baptising them in the name of the Father and the Son and the Holy Spirit. Teach these new disciples to obey all the commands I have given you. And be sure of this: I am with you always, even to the end of the age.

Matthew 28:19,20

Think of those you know who don't yet know Jesus and the power of his resurrection in their life.

How could you share more of that resurrection hope with them?

Prayer

Pray for those people you've just thought of who don't yet know Jesus, and for opportunities to share God's love with them over the next few weeks.

Groups might encourage each person to share one or two names so that you can pray for those people together. Is there some way you could continue to do that even though these sessions are ending?

Think about the events of Jesus' life that you've looked at over these sessions. Is there anything that you have found particularly thought-provoking or challenging over that time? If so, perhaps you could share that with others. Pray for one another and give thanks for the difference Jesus' life, death and resurrection has made to you.

End by reading these verses:

All honour to the God and Father of our Lord Jesus Christ, for it is by his boundless mercy that God has given us the privilege of being born again. Now we live with a wonderful expectation because Jesus Christ rose again from the dead. For God has reserved a priceless inheritance for his children. It is kept in heaven for you, pure and undefiled, beyond the reach of change and decay. And God, in his mighty power, will protect you until you receive this salvation, because you are trusting him. It will be revealed on the last day for all to see.

1 Peter 1:3–5

Further Afield

1 DOUBT AND CERTAINTY

Read

Matthew 28:16,17 and John 20:24–29

Q: Would you have trusted the word of your friends or would you have been like Thomas, needing to see the evidence yourself?

Q: Why do you think Thomas didn't trust the other disciples?

Q: Jesus didn't condemn Thomas for his doubts. Sometimes Christians are reluctant to admit to doubts. Why do you think that is?

Q: How do you think non-Christians would react if a Christian admitted they sometimes had doubts?

Q: Do you have doubts? If so, what do you do about them?

Q: Doubts can be hard to face. How could they help our faith to grow?

2 BEFORE AND AFTER

Read

Matthew 26:56b, Acts 12:1,2 and 1 Corinthians 15:3–7

Q: What were the disciples like before Jesus' death?

Afterwards they became people who spoke out bravely about Jesus. James wasn't the only one of the original 12 disciples to die for Jesus, just the first. Their obedience saw the gospel message shared and the church created.

Q: What made the difference?

Q: Our calling may be less dramatic but God still has a purpose for us. How are you serving God at the moment? Is there something different you could be doing?

Pray for God's power and wisdom in the areas of your life where you are serving God. Don't forget to include anywhere you are his representative, for example with your family, friends or colleagues.

3 OUR HOME IN HEAVEN

Read

2 Corinthians 5:1

Our true home is now in heaven. Spend some time thinking about what that means for you.

Q: What difference does that make to the way you live your life today?

Give thanks for that promise of a home in heaven and all that it means to you.

About the author

Kate Hayes, born into a non-churchgoing family in Sheffield, decided to become a Christian aged 12 after being 'dragged along' to a Pathfinder meeting by a friend. After studying psychology at university, she did teacher training, but then found herself working in bookshops and in software testing for the book trade. Since 1994 she's been in Dukinfield, Greater Manchester, where she coordinates and writes materials for small groups at St John's Church.

OTHER TITLES by KATE HAYES

A journey of the heart
A Pilgrim's Guide to Prayer
ISBN 1 85999 797 X

THE RE:ACTION SERIES – 6 SMALL GROUP RESOURCES

For the tough times
Does God care when I'm hurting?
ISBN 1 85999 622 1

Chosen for change
Am I part of God's big plan?
ISBN 1 85999 623 X

The possibility of purpose
What's the meaning of my life?
ISBN 1 85999 620 5

Jesus: the sequel
Is he really coming back?
ISBN 1 85999 621 3

More than fine words
Does my faith impact 24/7?
ISBN 1 85999 770 8

More than bricks and ritual
Am I a team player for God?
ISBN 1 85999 769 4

Available from all good Christian bookshops or from Scripture Union Mail Order: PO Box 5148, Milton Keynes MLO, MK2 2YX, tel 08450 706 006, or online through www.scriptureunion.org.uk